Over the Alps

The Mid Hants Railway in Colour

Published by Runpast Publishing, 10 Kingscote Grove, Cheltenham, Gloucestershire GL51 6JX.

ISBN 1 870754 65 4

Typesetting and reproduction by Viners Wood Associates. Printed in England by goodmanbaylis.

Introduction

The history of the railway line from Alton to Winchester can be traced back to 1845 when the London & South Western Railway (LSWR) undertook a survey of the countryside between the towns with a view to building a line to connect them. Nothing came of this proposal, however, no doubt to the intense disappointment of the residents of Alresford who wished their prosperous town to be served by the rapidly expanding rail network. In 1860 the scheme to construct a line was revived by the Alton, Alresford & Winchester Railway Company (AA&WR) and in November of that year a notice appeared in the *Hampshire Chronicle* stating that powers to build the line were being sought in the next session of Parliament. The first meeting of the directors took place at the Swan Hotel, Alresford, on 27th February 1861. The company's plans enjoyed considerable support from local people and members of both Houses of Parliament, so it probably came as no surprise when the AA&WR obtained its Act on 28th June 1861. Construction of the line started in 1863 and it eventually opened on 2nd October 1865, by which time the AA&WR had changed its name to the Mid Hants Railway Company (MHR). It was worked by the LSWR from the outset, the initial service consisting of four weekday passenger trains each way between Guildford and Southampton Terminus. In 1884, when the LSWR acquired the whole of the MHR's assets, one of its first steps was to increase the passenger service, which by this time formed part of a through secondary service from London to Southampton, to six trains in each direction on weekdays with two on Sundays and this level of service lasted well into Southern Railway (SR) days. The first tangible signs of the line's decline were seen in 1931 when the passing loops and signal boxes were removed from Itchen Abbas and Ropley. During the 1930s the SR had been pressing on with electrification and in July 1937 electric services commenced between Alton and Waterloo which brought enormous benefits for the majority of passengers. But electrification did not extend to the Mid Hants line whose passengers suffered further by losing their through services. The SR tried to pacify its customers by augmenting the service, but they could do little to hide the obvious plight of the line, which had been reduced overnight from a secondary route with through London services to that of a sleepy country branch.

During the Second World War the route saw heavy troop train traffic, but in the early 1950s the line's slow decline continued as competition from the private car intensified. In 1957, however, BR embarked on the dieselisation of services in Hampshire using 2-car diesel-electric units and these brought about a change, albeit temporary, in the Mid Hants line's fortunes. On 4th November of that year a new hourly service was introduced between Alton and Southampton and as a result both passenger journeys and receipts showed a substantial increase. Local people doubtless hoped that the new, improved service would be the route's salvation but, alas, they were wrong. The line was proposed for closure in the infamous Beeching Report and the first statutory closure notices appeared in 1967 (stating that it was proposed to close the line from 6th May 1968), thus marking the start of an epic struggle between the local authorities and passenger groups on the one hand and monolithic BR on the other. One thousand objections were made to the closure and two public inquiries were necessary, one in 1968 and another in 1970. Objectors were enraged by some of the financial information about the route concocted by BR and the Department of the Environment, which stated that the line cost £135,000 per annum to run, but had annual income of only £31,000. The latter figure was allegedly based on an expected increase of 7% in passenger journeys which was in stark contrast to the estimate of a 144% surge in passengers calculated by the groups fighting the closure. Meanwhile, whilst the legal wrangles were making the headlines, BR were reducing many of the line's facilities to the bare minimum, almost as if they were deliberately trying to drive away as many passengers as possible. It was a very sad day when, on 25th August 1971, the Secretary of State for the Environment announced that his department was to allow BR to shut the line. Two further inquiries into the suitability of replacement bus services were forced by the objectors, but it was all in vain and the last trains ran on 4th February 1973.

But not all of the Alton to Winchester line was to die and, indeed, a new and glorious chapter in the history of the line was about to commence. The first moves towards preservation had already been made in 1972 and following the closure members of the Mid Hants Railway Limited took over the station area and signal box at Alresford, whilst Hampshire County Council agreed to pay BR £13,650 per annum to keep the track *in situ*. The Winchester & Alton Railway Company was formed in May 1973 to spearhead the rescue operation supported by the Mid Hants Railway Preservation Society. Years of endeavour and commitment were rewarded on 21st March 1977 when a Light Railway Order was granted by the government – the society had won through! Amidst great celebration the stretch of line from Alresford to Ropley was re-opened by the chairman of Hampshire County Council on 30th April 1977, the first train being hauled by N Class No.31874. The year 1980 saw the completion of the engine shed at Ropley, whilst other milestones during that year were the final payment to BR for the track between Alresford and Ropley and the alterations to the track layout at Alton to accommodate Mid Hants trains in anticipation of the reinstatement of the line from Ropley. The section as far as Medstead & Four Marks was relaid in the second half of 1982 with services being resumed on 28th May 1983. The bulk of the track laying on the final stretch from there to Alton took place between November 1984 and February 1985. The work was carried out from the Alton end, very often in appalling weather conditions, and the final track panel was laid to complete the link on 12th April 1985. The first Mid Hants train steamed into Alton on 25th May 1985. Mission accomplished – another great achievement!

I would like to express my appreciation to all of the talented photographers who kindly provided their precious, irreplaceable transparencies for a much wider audience to enjoy. In addition, Chris Evans, David J. Fakes, James Knights, Graham Mallinson and Chris Small have perused the manuscript and suggested many amendments and improvements. I accept responsibility for any inaccuracies that remain.

M. S. W., Burgess Hill, West Sussex, September 2005

The introduction of diesel working on the Southampton to Alton service from 4th November 1957 ensured that the local steam passenger services along the Mid Hants line were very little photographed in colour. In fact, the passenger trains on the route were among the first on the Southern Region (SR) to be modernised, as part of the Hampshire dieselisation scheme. Consequently, very few images from the 1950s are known to exist and it must be admitted that this picture has been published before. In this illustration of considerable historical importance, M7 Class 0-4-4T No.30125 is seen at Itchen Abbas station with an Alton to Southampton push-pull train on an unknown date in 1957. This particular locomotive was transferred to Eastleigh shed in 1939 and proved to be one of the longest serving members of its class on the Mid Hants line. The push-pull service dated from the introduction of electric trains east of Alton in July 1937 and prior to that time the Mid Hants line had been served by through services from Waterloo to Eastleigh/Southampton. When the electric trains started the Alton to Winchester line found itself on the fringe of the electrified area and its status was downgraded from a secondary line served by through trains to little more than a sleepy branch line with a purely local service.

Neil Sprinks

A view of Medstead & Four Marks station in 1957 with 700 Class 0-6-0 No.30350 pausing in charge of an up (Alton-bound) freight train. Locomotives of this class based at Eastleigh shed virtually monopolised freight working along the Mid Hants line in the very early 1950s, but were largely replaced by Maunsell Q Class 0-6-0s in about 1953. In 1956, however, the 700 Class staged a comeback when the workings were altered as a result of the deteriorating condition of Alton's turntable, which was taken out of use. From that time Guildford shed became responsible for working both the up and down daily freights, the locomotive powering the Alton local trip freights continuing to Eastleigh where it stabled on the shed overnight. It returned to Guildford in charge of the following day's up Mid Hants line freight. Guildford shed had a fair complement of 700 Class locomotives which regularly appeared on these turns. No.30350 was an Eastleigh-based engine until 1953 when it was transferred to Guildford so it continued to be seen at Alton. In 1959 the freight workings were reduced to thrice-weekly and ceased altogether on 21st May 1964 when Q1 Class 0-6-0 No.33036 worked the final train from Medstead to Alton. Coal trains continued to Treloars Hospital, on the outskirts of Alton, until July 1967. Goods traffic to Farringdon, on the former Meon Valley line, lasted until August 1968. *Neil Sprinks*

Photographed from the cab of an M7 Class 0-4-4T hauling the 8.55am Alton to Eastleigh local train, Class LN 'Lord Nelson' 4-6-0 No.30862 *Lord Collingwood* waits in the up platform at Medstead & Four Marks station with a troop train on 28th May 1957. The Mid Hants line was the ideal route for conveying troops between Aldershot and Southampton Docks and was very heavily used for this purpose during both world wars. The 'Lord Nelsons' were a small class which became extinct (apart from a preserved example) in the early 1960s and, therefore, pictures of these locomotives working along the Mid Hants line are not plentiful: this is the only colour shot known to the author. The class appeared sporadically over the years and other workings included No.30861 *Lord Anson*, which powered a troop train on 3rd January 1957, while 5th January 1961 saw no fewer than three 'Lord Nelsons' hauling Ocean Liner boat trains over the line following a serious earth slip at Hook on the main Waterloo to Bournemouth line.

S.C. Townroe/Colour-Rail

Right, above: A stranger on the Mid Hants line! In June 1959 the first part of the Kent Coast electrification scheme was inaugurated and many steam locomotives were displaced, being withdrawn or moved to other sheds. A remarkable feature of the motive power changes that occurred at this time was nominal transfer of no less than 106 former Eastern Section engines to Nine Elms shed in London. It is unlikely that all of these machines actually reached their new home and some were noted dumped out of use, probably never to work again. Some of the locomotives in good condition were found employment at Nine Elms, however, and these more fortunate engines included L Class 4-4-0 No.31768, which was doubtless put to use on a variety of mundane duties including empty stock workings and the occasional van train, in between periods in store. On 18th September 1960 No.31768 was used on a Locomotive Club of Great Britain (LCGB) rail tour over the Alton to Winchester line and is seen here at the eastern approach to Alresford cutting. Using different motive power, the tour later visited the Fawley branch and the Brockenhurst to Broadstone line via Ringwood. The return journey to London was via Templecombe and Salisbury – no doubt a wonderful day out over some really interesting routes! *Colour-Rail*

Right, below: When the main Waterloo to Bournemouth line was blocked by planned engineering operations or emergencies the Mid Hants line was often used for diversionary purposes and the diverted services naturally included the famous 'Bournemouth Belle' Pullman car train. Almost needless to say, Pullman cars were not normally seen on the Alton to Winchester line! In this shot, taken at the same location as the previous picture near Alresford, the down 'Belle' is seen with Bulleid 'Merchant Navy' Class Pacific No.35018 *British India Line* being piloted by U Class 'Mogul' No.31628. The train was being diverted as a result of the earthslip at Hook and this shot was taken on 8th January 1961. *B.J. Swain/Colour-Rail*

In the 1960s prior to the end of Southern Region steam, hardly a weekend seemed to go by without a rail tour being run to commemorate the extinction of a well-known class of locomotive or closure of a branch line. Societies vied with each other to produce the most appealing itineraries and the steeply-graded Mid Hants line, where all services were usually diesel operated, was included if at all possible. This picture of Urie-designed S15 Class No.30512 climbing out of Alton with an LCGB rail tour was taken on 3rd November 1963.

This was the last day the Hayling Island branch was open for traffic (the last day of public services being 2nd November) and the main purpose of the special was to give participants a final trip along this short, but very distinctive line. In order to make the day even more interesting the tour also included the Portsmouth dockyard and Lavant branches. The tour concluded with a run up the scenic Mid-Sussex line (as it was then known) to London Victoria with a pair of Maunsell Q Class locomotives as motive power. *Chris Small*

This illustration shows the 10.30am Waterloo to Weymouth train descending the bank between Medstead & Four Marks and Ropley on 8th December 1963 with BRCW Type 3 Bo-Bo No.D6532 piloting Bulleid 'Merchant Navy' Class Pacific No.35024 *East Asiatic Company*. There were engineering works on that day between Fleet and Winchfield involving the renewal of a bridge and the Type 3 had previously piloted the 9.33am Waterloo to Bournemouth West train south of Alton as booked. Unfortunately, owing to the very icy conditions the work over-ran and the 10.30am train, which had been scheduled to travel on its normal route was also diverted, but no pilot was available for the climb out of Alton and the train had to wait 70 minutes for assistance while No.D6532 was summoned from Winchester.   *John Langford*

The train service between Southampton Terminus and Alton was (as previously mentioned) one of the first in the south of England to be dieselised, diesel electric multiple units (DEMUs) taking over from steam traction on 4th November 1957. Average journey times between those points were reduced by up to 22min. and dieselisation of the Hampshire lines generally, which produced a 29% leap in patronage, was hailed as a huge commercial success by BR. The introduction of the new units went reasonably smoothly, but problems arose on the Mid Hants line in the autumn of 1959 when, as a result of traffic growth, the 2-car units were augmented to 3-cars which were soon in trouble on the route's 1 in 60 gradients. There was a hasty reversion to 2-cars in November 1959, 3-car units being re-introduced during the following month after some units had had their express gear ratio bogies replaced with those fitted with suburban gear ratio. From the winter 1960 timetable, however, the line was diagrammed to be worked predominantly by 2-car units, the middle trailer being removed at random from any two units at a time for the Mid Hants line service. In May 1964 2-car unit No.1122, which had been built in 1958 for use on East Sussex/Kent branches, was permanently transferred from St. Leonards to Eastleigh specifically for use on the Alton line and in December of the same year sister unit No.1121 followed. These two units then worked the Mid Hants route until closure in 1973, apart from occasions when they were undergoing maintenance. In this classic view unit No.1122 is seen near Mount Pleasant road bridge, on the outskirts of Alton, with the 9.53am Southampton Terminus to Alton train on 30th August 1965.   *Chris Small*

The up platform at Medstead & Four Marks station is depicted in this picture which was taken on 9th January 1966. This station was opened three years after passenger services commenced on the Alton to Winchester line and this may account for the more modest facilities provided compared to the other stations on the line. During the first years of the station's existence the stationmaster is thought to have been a Mr. Grimbley, who moved to Cobham in 1884. In 1879 a shelter on the down side was constructed and further improvements took place in 1901 when the loop line and platform were extended. In the 1920s, before motor transport had begun to make a real impact on rural life, Medstead station was still a vital lifeline to people in the surrounding area. There was milk and livestock traffic and an occasional basket of pigeons would arrive to be set free for training flights. The station also dealt with agricultural machinery, builders' supplies and stock for the local nurseries. In 1937 the premises were renamed 'Medstead & Four Marks'. In more recent times the block post was abolished in 1967 and the signal box demolished two years later.

Roger Merry-Price

The exhaust steam being emitted by Maunsell S15 Class 4-6-0 No.30837 makes a magnificent sight as it hangs in the cold, still, winter air. This picture of the LCGB's 'S15 Commemorative Rail Tour' was taken on 9th January 1966 and shows the train ascending Medstead Bank in fine style. No.30837 was specially retained by the SR to work a farewell special after the other remaining members of the class had been condemned, and Feltham shed turned out the locomotive in absolutely sparkling condition, as seen here. In the event, the tour was considerably over subscribed and two trains ran on consecutive Sundays, the train seen here being the relief working. By the following Sunday the countryside had been blanketed by a heavy snowfall and the train was assisted over the 'Alps' (as the Alton to Winchester line was known) by a Maunsell 'Mogul'. Sadly, despite its magnificent displays, No.30837 was later broken up for scrap – what a waste!

Alan Chandler

In a scene that was repeated many times during the mid-1960s, BRCW Type 3 1,550hp Bo-Bo No.D6556 backs down onto the front of the 'Bournemouth Belle' at Alton station on 24th April 1966. Judging by the steam escaping from the safety valves, the fireman of Bulleid Pacific No.34017 *Ilfracombe* has already built up boiler pressure for the hard work that lies ahead. Another BRCW Type 3 can be seen in the distance, no doubt awaiting the call to pilot a following train over the Mid Hants line. Other performers on diverted trains on the same day included No.34060 *25 Squadron* on the 10.30am ex-Waterloo, which apparently did not take a pilot, and No.35022 *Holland-America Line* in charge of the 8.30pm Waterloo to Bournemouth Central, which also appears to have been unassisted.

Colour-Rail

Two heads of steam are better than one! The 9.33am from Waterloo to Bournemouth train, hauled by BR Standard Class 5MT 4-6-0 No.73169 piloting Bulleid 'Battle of Britain' Class Pacific No.34077 *603 Squadron*, approaches Butts Junction on 1st May 1966. Unfortunately, the locomotives are in absolutely filthy condition, but even so make an impressive sight. This train doubtless conveyed many 'day trippers' visiting Bournemouth and other Hampshire coast resorts, so was probably a very heavy working. At least the sun was shining when they passed through Alton! The following four illustrations were also taken on 1st May 1966 and give a remarkable insight into the types of trains and motive power that could be seen on the Mid Hants route when it was being used for diversionary purposes. Three overnight trains (not photographed!) produced Bulleid Pacifics, whilst the 2.25am Waterloo to Poole was powered by 'Warship' diesel No.D870 *Zulu*. It should be noted that the Mid Hants route and former Meon Valley line (in the foreground) were operated as two independent single lines, hence the apparent 'wrong line working' in this shot.

Chris Small

Right, above: After the double-headed 9.33am *ex-*Waterloo had passed there would have been a lull until the 10.30am from Waterloo to Weymouth appeared with 'Merchant Navy' Class Pacific No.35008 *Orient Line* at its head. Despite its very heavy load the Pacific climbed Medstead bank single-handed. In the foreground a carpet of bluebells enhances the scene. *Orient Line* remained active almost to the end of SR steam, working a BR 'Farewell to SR Steam' special from Waterloo to Weymouth and return on 2nd July 1967. It worked various other services during the last week of steam traction, but was later cut-up for scrap.　*Alan Chandler*

Right, below: Another illustration of the 10.30am Waterloo to Weymouth train, this time showing *Orient Line* 'blowing off' as it approaches Medstead & Four Marks station. Bulleid Pacific boilers were noted for their prodigious steaming capacity, although it must be admitted that some aspects of the original design proved to be something of a fitter's 'nightmare'. Note Medstead signal box's down distant signal on the right.　*Roger Merry-Price*

In a further shot taken on 1st May 1966 the 11.30am Waterloo to Weymouth train, headed by Bulleid 'West Country' Pacific No.34002 *Salisbury*, heads out of Alton and starts the climb towards Medstead. The three-arch overbridge in the background carries Mount Pleasant (a suburban road) across the railway. Note the track here, the 'main' Mid Hants line being laid on concrete sleepers at this point, whilst the old Meon Valley line, which was still open for freight traffic as far as Farringdon, has most unusual steel sleepers. There does not appear to be a wooden sleeper in sight! *Salisbury*, the oldest surviving unrebuilt Bulleid 'Light Pacific', was originally scheduled for preservation by the British Transport Commission. When No.34051 *Winston Churchill* hauled Sir Winston's funeral train in January 1965 it was felt more appropriate to preserve the latter engine and, sadly, No.34002 went for scrap.

Chris Small

In addition to No.34002 *Salisbury* on the 11.30am Waterloo to Weymouth train, a second unrebuilt Bulleid Pacific worked over the Mid Hants line on 1st May 1966. This was No.34019 *Bideford* which was in charge of the 4.30pm from Waterloo to Weymouth, so photographers who particularly liked unmodified Bulleid Pacifics would have been rewarded by two possible pictures, provided they were prepared to wait! By this date unrebuilt locomotives were becoming a little thin on the ground, so two examples in a day on diverted trains was quite a treat for photographers. In this view *Bideford* is seen near Hampshire Hunt bridge which was originally built for the convenience of local huntsmen who paid an annual levy to the railway for its use.

Roger Merry-Price

Left, above: During the latter days of South Western Division (SWD) main line steam the York to Poole through train was rostered for a London Midland Region Class 5MT between Banbury and Poole from February 1966. This train did not operate on Sundays so the incoming locomotive normally remained on Bournemouth shed from the Saturday evening to the Monday morning and was available for special traffic duties as required. On 15th May 1966 the main line was due to be blocked by engineering works and the SWD's engine diagrams staff, who apparently included one or two enthusiasts, had suggested to the photographer that it might be a good idea(!) for him to look out for the 8.55am Bournemouth Central to Waterloo which was scheduled to run via the Mid Hants line. To the photographer's surprise the train appeared behind Stanier 'Black Five' No.45493, which is depicted here passing Butts Junction. The same locomotive was used on this train the following Sunday but, regrettably, this was the last time the train ran via Alton thus denying the line any further 'foreign' visitors. In years gone by a number of these machines worked over the line, especially during the SR's motive power crisis in 1953, which was precipitated by the discovery of fractured driving axles on 'Merchant Navy' Class engines. *Chris Small*

Left, below: The 9.54am Weymouth to Waterloo train passes Ropley on 15th May 1966. Motive power is provided by Bulleid 'Light Pacific' No.34019 *Bideford* piloted by BR Standard Class 4MT 2-6-4T No.80151: the latter engine is currently preserved on the Bluebell Railway. The Mid Hants Railway's locomotive works has since been constructed on the land in the foreground and the view seen here has changed dramatically. Ropley station building dominates the background. Note the third and fourth vehicles in the train which appear to be dining and restaurant cars respectively: both have solebar fairings, which indicate that they were originally built in 1947 at Eastleigh Carriage Works as part of eleven six-car rakes for use on the Waterloo to Bournemouth services.
Roy Hobbs

Right, above: On the following Sunday, 22nd May 1966, the 9.54am Weymouth to Waterloo was once again double-headed using a BR Standard Class 4MT 2-6-4T as the pilot locomotive. On this occasion the train engine was 'Merchant Navy' Pacific No.35029 *Ellerman Lines* with Standard tank No.80139 as the leading engine. The train has just passed Ropley station, which is on a gradient of 1 in 250 thus providing a very brief respite from the ruling 1 in 80 gradient which applies on each side of the station. However, about a mile beyond Ropley the incline steepens to 1 in 60 which continues unabated until Medstead & Four Marks station is reached. The pilot engine would have worked only as far as Alton and returned to Eastleigh 'light engine'. After a long period languishing at Barry scrapyard *Ellerman Lines* was acquired by the National Railway Museum and sectioned for display purposes at York Museum. *Roger Merry-Price*

Right, below: After the end of the train heating season there was no longer a requirement for trains to be heated and more diesels started to appear on diverted services, thus robbing the Mid Hants line of much interest. There were usually sufficient steam locomotives in use to keep the steam enthusiasts happy, however, but one train they definitely would have avoided was the 1.30pm Waterloo to Weymouth which was double-headed over the Alton to Winchester section by BRCW Type 3 No.D6517 and Brush Type 4 Co-Co No.D1683 on 5th June. The pair are seen here climbing out of Alton with a lot of work ahead of them before the summit is reached at Medstead & Four Marks. *Chris Small*

Despite the overcast conditions, not to mention the grimy state of the locomotive, BR Standard Class 5MT No.73171 still manages to create a stirring image as it climbs away from Alton with the 11.30am Waterloo to Weymouth train on 12th June 1966. Part of Alton station is just visible in the background. The exit from Alton is on the modest gradient (by Mid Hants line standards!) of 1 in 100 and there is even a very brief level section just before the site of Butts Junction. After that the incline steepens dramatically to a very challenging 1 in 60 which applies until Medstead & Four Marks station is reached.   *Roy Hobbs*

In normal circumstances, as previously mentioned, passenger services along the Mid Hants line were formed of 2-car 'Hampshire' units based at Eastleigh maintenance depot, unit Nos.1121 and 1122 being specifically allocated for this service. Occasionally, an infiltrator would appear, often as a result of a unit visiting Eastleigh Works being commandeered by Eastleigh depot before it returned home. In this picture 3D 'Oxted' unit No.1312 is seen forming the 3.53pm Alton to Portsmouth & Southsea train on 29th July 1966. The unit is in pristine external condition following repair at Eastleigh Works and was presumably waiting to return to its home depot of St. Leonards. Note the inverted black triangle on the cab front: this indicated to platform staff that the guard's brake was positioned at that end of the formation. Other 'Oxted' units have been recorded on the Alton to Winchester line, plus some second class only 3R 'Tadpole' units.   *Chris Small*

Left, above: The incredible sight of BR Standard Class 3MT 2-6-0 No.77014 piloting unrebuilt 'West Country' Pacific No.34102 *Lapford* on the diverted 'Bournemouth Belle' must surely rank as one of the most remarkable combinations of motive power seen on the Alton to Winchester line in BR days. This unlikely pair is seen heaving the 'Belle' up Medstead bank on 18th September 1966. The unsightly mess on No.77014's smokebox door was reportedly caused by rain partially washing off a chalked headcode disc! The Class 3MT also piloted two other services on the same day. No.77014 was one of twenty engines initially shared between the Scottish and North Eastern regions, but No.77014 migrated southwards to Northwich in 1964. It was first noted on the SR in March 1966 and was officially allocated to Guildford from 2nd April. It is likely that this unprecedented pairing was specially arranged by steam enthusiasts in the former Divisional Manager's Office at Wimbledon, doubtless with the collusion of the relevant shed foremen. *Roy Hobbs*

Left, below: The 10.30am Waterloo to Weymouth train, headed by BRCW Type 3 Bo-Bo No.D6540, has just passed underneath Borovere Lane bridge and approaches Butts Junction on 18th June 1967. By this date the introduction of full electric working on the Bournemouth Line was less than a month away and some trains were comprised of 3TC/4TC units that had been formed to operate the new service. These units were mainly designed to operate with the high-powered '4 Rep' electric units, but could also be worked in a push-pull mode by either a specially converted BRCW Type 3 or an electro-diesel locomotive. In addition, they could be hauled in conventional style by a standard Type 3, as seen here. The train depicted was formed of 4TC unit Nos.416, 425 and 403: taking such a heavy load over the 'Alps' would have represented quite a challenge for the moderately powered BRCW Type 3. *Chris Small*

A hill near the hamlet of Chawton provides an excellent panoramic viewpoint for this shot of the 'Bournemouth Belle' climbing Medstead bank behind Brush 2,750hp Type 4 No.D1685 on New Year's Day 1967; the main A31 road is partially concealed by trees in the foreground. By this date more diverted services were being diesel-worked and the wonderful spectacle of steam traction being worked to the limit on these trains was becoming a thing of the past. For example on this day the only steam locomotive observed was Bulleid 'Battle of Britain' Pacific No.34071 *601 Squadron* powering the 11.35pm (Saturday night) Waterloo to Bournemouth train which actually ran only as far as Southampton due to further work along the line: all other diverted trains were hauled by BRCW Type 3s, Brush Type 4s or 'Warship' locomotives. The very last steam-hauled diverted train ran on 11th June 1967 when No.34093 *Saunton* appeared on the 9.33am Waterloo to Bournemouth, thus ending a particularly interesting chapter in the history of the Alton to Winchester line.   *Trevor Owen*

A Southampton Central to Alton train, formed of 3H 'Hampshire' DEMU No.1101 approaches Alresford station some time in the late summer of 1971. Since this picture was taken this location has changed out of all recognition and much of the land seen here is now occupied by sidings used for rolling stock storage. Mercifully, the old goods shed (partially visible on the right) remains and has recently been refurbished, finding a new lease of life principally as the MHR's bookshop. Trains were booked to cross here and it is likely that another 3H was also in the vicinity of Alresford. Unit No.1101 originally entered service as a 2-car unit in September 1957 and was augmented to 3-car in October 1959. It was destined to have a remarkably long career and survived on Uckfield line services, once again running as a 2-car unit, until late 2004.

Marcus Eavis

A fascinating view of the country end of Alton station in early 1973, shortly before the cessation of passenger services along the Alton to Winchester line. A 3H DEMU, doubtless bound for Southampton, already has 'the road' and is ticking over in the middle platform prior to leaving on the first stage of its journey to Medstead & Four Marks. A '4 Vep' is also visible on the right, presumably with a train to Waterloo. The track layout at Alton underwent considerable modification in the mid-1930s resulting from the abolition of Butts Junction signal box on 18th February 1935 and to prepare it for its new role as the limit of electric working from London. The Alton to Butts section was converted to parallel single lines. Platform 1, the original up main line, was extended at the London end to accommodate 8-car formations, while Platform 2, the old up loop, became the platform for Mid Hants trains. Platform 3, the former down main, was used by the Meon Valley line trains. However, further changes had occurred by the date of this picture, Platforms 1 and 3 being used by electric trains whilst Platform 2 was disconnected at the London end of the station and was the sole preserve of the DEMUs.   *Gerald Daniels*

A copy of BR's official closure notice is prominent in this photograph taken at Alton station on 3rd February 1973, the penultimate day of services on the Mid Hants line. 3H DEMU No.1121 awaits departure in Platform 2 with the next train to Southampton. Closure of the line was originally proposed in the Beeching Report and, not surprisingly, the threat to the line sparked uproar among local people; about a thousand objections to the closure were received by the Transport Users Consultative Committee (TUCC) and a public inquiry was held in Alresford in April 1968. BR stated that annual earnings were £50,000 and expenses £70,900 and that about £65,000 was needed to be spent on track renewals between 1968 and 1972. Protestors gained a temporary reprieve, but in July 1970 a further inquiry was held in Winchester. It was stated by objectors that new building development was leading to increasing traffic on the route and they questioned the ability of the local bus company to carry the extra passengers, but it was all to no avail and on 1st December 1972 the Government announced the final death sentence. *Gerald Daniels*

Right above: Itchen Abbas was by far the least photographed of the Mid Hants line stations and consequently very few pictures were submitted for inclusion in this album. The premises were becoming rather overgrown and neglected when this shot was taken from a passing train on 30th October 1971. Originally known as Itchen Abbotts, the station was the quietest on the route and served only the village of Itchen Abbas and the nearby hamlet of Avington. When built, the station had a passing loop and signal box but these were removed in 1931. The tiny goods yard consisted of just one long siding and a dock siding, both of which were accessed from a headshunt: the yard was closed in 1962. Latterly the station had been staffed by one man, but he was pensioned off in 1965 when conductor guards were introduced on the trains. Following closure the entire site was auctioned and a housing estate now stands where trains once ran.

Tom Pettle collection/MHR archives

Right below: Alresford station appears to be exceptionally busy in this picture, but photographs can sometimes be deceptive! This shot was actually taken on Sunday 4th February 1973, the last day of services between Alton and Winchester, and shows mourners gathered on the platforms. Many were no doubt intending to make a final journey over the line. One wonders how many of those pictured anticipated that thirty years later it would still be possible to travel by train from Alresford to Alton!

Tom Pettle collection/MHR archives

The long campaign to save the line from extinction had brought together many people and some were determined to restore services if at all possible. They vowed to fight on! The first preservation group was the Mid Hants Railway Limited which was formed in 1972. In May 1973 the Winchester & Alton Railway Company (W&AR), which was supported by the Mid Hants Railway Preservation Society, came into being and Hampshire County Council agreed to pay a year's rent to secure the retention of the permanent way. This was subsequently extended until the W&AR was in a position to purchase.

Unfortunately a share offer in May 1975, which was intended to save the entire 17 miles-long route, failed to reach the minimum legal subscription, but a second share offer six months later succeeded. This had the more modest objective of preserving the Alresford to Alton section and a deposit was paid on the three miles of track from Alresford to Ropley. In the meantime a couple of industrial locomotives arrived and are just visible in the background of this picture of Alresford which was taken on a frosty day in early 1974.

Klaus Marx

The year 1976 proved to be another eventful one in the history of the MHR. On 6th March 1976 four coaches and a parcels van were delivered by rail. This was the last train to be worked over the line by BR and track lifting commenced on either side of the preserved Alresford to Ropley section. On a happier note four steam locomotives arrived in 1976 to join N Class No.31874, an earlier acquisition. The next major landmark in the line's history was on 21st March 1977 when the W&AR obtained its Light Railway Order and a few weeks later the culmination of years of effort were rewarded when H.M. Inspector gave his approval for services to commence. There was great celebration when the line reopened on 30th April 1977 and in this shot, taken on 21st May, Hunslet 'Austerity' 0-6-0ST No.196 is seen piloting No.31874.				*David Clark*

Another view of No.196, this time showing the locomotive running complete with its *Errol Lonsdale* nameplates. This picture was taken when it was hauling the 4.05pm Ropley to Alresford train on 23rd April 1978. Nos.196 and 31874 (then named *Aznar Line*) were the only working locomotives during 1978, and bore the brunt of operations until *Bodmin* became available in September 1979. No.196 was built by the Hunslet Engine Co. in 1953, one of a batch of fifteen constructed as a war reserve: it was stored at the Ministry of Defence, Liphook (Hampshire) until 1955. It was moved from there to Honeybourne, Warwickshire, and was subsequently transferred to the nearby Long Marston Supplies Depot. In 1964 it was moved again, this time to the Longmoor Military Railway entering traffic in 1965, and later appeared in various films, including *The Great St. Trinian's Train Robbery*, which was filmed on the Longmoor Military Railway in 1965. No.196 was named in 1967 but, following the closure of the Longmoor complex, this nomadic engine was on the move yet again. In 1970 it was bought for private preservation on the Kent & East Sussex Railway until being purchased for use on the MHR in 1976. At the time of writing this locomotive is based at Buckfastleigh, on the South Devon Railway.

John Scrace

Right above: In this portrait Maunsell N Class 'Mogul' No.31874 is depicted waiting to leave Ropley station with the 6.05pm to Alresford on 16th July 1978. The 'Mogul' was, as previously mentioned, one of only two engines available for traffic during that year so this must have been a very common sight at that time! Note that the last three vehicles in the train are BR-designed high capacity non-corridor carriages which had recently been displaced from King's Cross suburban services. No.31874 was manufactured at Woolwich Arsenal shortly after the First World War and purchased at a bargain price by the Southern Railway in 1924 when it was still only partially assembled. After completion at Ashford Works it entered traffic as No.A874 in 1925, based at Bricklayers Arms shed in London. During its career it saw service at many sheds, including spells at Guildford, Eastleigh and Exmouth Junction. In October 1961 31874 became one of the last of its class to receive a general overhaul: final withdrawal came on 17th March 1964 and it was sent to Barry scrapyard. No.31874 arrived at the MHR on 16th March 1974 and was the first main line locomotive to arrive at the railway. Restoration was carried out at an incredible pace and its fire was lit for the first time in preservation on 3rd October 1976. The engine carried the name *Aznar Line* for a while, was renamed *Brian Fisk* on 15th September 1979, but is not named at the time of writing.   *John Scrace*

Right below: A picture of Ropley station in early 1980 when it was still the limit of operations. The station was probably most famous for its impressive topiary which was in the course of being reinstated when this shot was taken. The skeleton of the MHR locomotive works is visible in the background. The main station building was built to the standard Mid Hants pattern and designed to include residential accommodation in addition to the usual passenger facilities. The station is in a quiet location with only a few dwellings nearby, the village of Ropley being a mile away to the south-east. At the time of this picture the premises had been restored in LSWR colours and the dedicated restoration work undertaken there was officially recognised with a 'Best Preserved Station' award in 1981. Today the station boasts a footbridge, which was obtained from North Tawton on the Exeter to Barnstaple line, and a signal box from Netley, Hampshire. The station has subsequently been repainted in 'Southern' colours.

Klaus Marx

Hauling a rake of six BR Standard Mk.I coaches, including a buffet car, Maunsell U Class 2-6-0 No.31806 creates a stirring image near Bishops Sutton as it climbs towards Ropley on Boxing Day 1982. This locomotive was originally built at Brighton Works in October 1926 as one of the ill-fated 'River' K Class 2-6-4Ts and was named *River Torridge*. These machines were notoriously rough riding and after the Sevenoaks disaster in 1927 a decision was taken to rebuild all twenty locomotives as U Class tender engines. No.806 was rebuilt over a period of three months at Brighton and emerged on 21st June 1928: it was renumbered 1806 in 1932. During an unremarkable working life No.1806 (later BR No.31806) was allocated to various sheds, the locomotive's final depot being Guildford from where it worked Reading to Redhill trains. Withdrawal came in January 1964, the engine having covered 970,103 miles in service. It was consigned to Barry, but rescue came in June 1975 and 31806 eventually re-entered service in April 1981.

Tony Eaton

A railway revived. After more than ten years of disuse and dereliction Medstead & Four Marks station was on the brink of opening a new chapter in its history when this photograph was taken on 23rd April 1983. New track had been laid and newly repainted 'barley sugar' lamp standards plus white platform edges suggest that life was returning. It is probably true to say that one could write a book about Medstead station's restoration! The site had become the haunt of local vandals and in 1980 replacement of the station by a bus type shelter was seriously suggested. Major reconstruction work was needed on the main building which was little more than a shell: this included the rebuilding of interior walls and the laying of a concrete floor in the booking office. Other substantial work included rebuilding the main chimneystack and replacing all of the damaged roof slates. When track laying commenced thoughts turned to the return of regular trains and the urgent need for a signal box. Negotiations opened with BR for the redundant box at Wilton South, near Salisbury, and this arrived in October 1982. The early part of 1983 saw drainage being installed for the main building and work on the electricity supply. When the premises opened for business on 28th May 1983 only the booking hall was finished, but that was an achievement in itself. The dedicated work undertaken at Medstead has since been officially recognised by its success in the 1998 'Best Restored Station' competition. *Klaus Marx*

Maunsell U Class 'Mogul' No.31806 may never have been in the limelight in ordinary service, but it certainly was the focus of attention entering Medstead & Four Marks station on 29th May 1983. This was only the second day of operation following the restoration of services on the Ropley to Medstead section, hence the groups of curious onlookers and colourful bunting. The unrestored down platform, bereft of any buildings, can be seen in the foreground. Since this photograph was taken a huge amount of work has been carried out at Medstead station to restore the premises to their former appearance, including the construction of a waiting room on the down platform. Another very creditable achievement is the erection of a footbridge, from Cowes station on the Isle of Wight. The track at the country end of Medstead station is one of the very few level sections between Alton and Alresford, but just beyond the platform ends the gradient changes, as illustrated here.

David Cox

The beautiful LSWR T9 Class 4-4-0 No.30120 is surely the most elegant locomotive ever to have graced the tracks of the MHR! This superb engine is depicted near Bishops Sutton in October 1983 and makes an unforgettable sight in the autumn sunshine. Sixty-six of these machines were built to the design of Dugald Drummond between 1899 and 1901, No.120 being one of the first batch built at Nine Elms: it entered service in August 1899. Due to their free-running capabilities the locomotives were commonly known to enginemen as 'Greyhounds'. They were built for express passenger work, but in the late 1920s were largely ousted from these duties by larger, more powerful locomotives. The T9s were then modified with superheaters and extended smokeboxes and found themselves in a new role as secondary express engines. No.30120 spent long periods shedded at both Eastleigh and Fratton depots amongst others, and earned a place in history when it powered the final passenger train from Newbury to Eastleigh on 5th March 1960. Like many of the last T9s its career finished in the West Country, being withdrawn in June 1961. But the locomotive was restored in LSWR light green livery and re-entered traffic in March 1962 mostly working enthusiasts' specials. On final withdrawal in June 1963 it became part of the National Collection and entered service on the MHR in May 1983. It was later repainted in SR green and saw some use on the Swanage Railway before retirement from active operation. At the time of writing it is on static display at the Bluebell Railway.

Tony Eaton

In this picture, another shot taken in glorious autumn sunshine, BR Standard Class 4MT 2-6-0 No.76017 storms through Bighton Lane cutting with an eastbound train on 27th October 1984. This location, between Alresford and Ropley, near the hamlet of Bishops Sutton, is a favourite spot for lineside photographers because the line runs in a south-easterly direction for a short time, thus providing photographic opportunities not available at other locations.

Roger Cruse

During the Second World War an 'Austerity' version of the Stanier 8F Class was produced for the Ministry of Supply under the direction of Mr. R.A. Riddles, and the WD 2-8-0s eventually totalled 935 machines. To enable running on lightly laid track a 2-10-0 version was also produced and 150 locomotives were constructed. The engines were used extensively overseas and were extremely successful: they had an axle loading of only 13 1/2 tons yet developed a tractive effort of 34,215lbs. The locomotive depicted here was built by the North British Locomotive Co. of Glasgow in 1943 and became WD No.73652. In 1944 it was among sixteen WD 2-10-0s sent to Greece and was later bought by the Hellenic State Railway, becoming their No.951. In the late 1970s the MHR identified Greece as a possible source of large locomotives in good condition and a party of members journeyed to Athens. Red tape, a general election in Greece and alleged lack of communication within Greek Railways conspired to cause interminable delays and it was 1984 before the go-ahead to purchase was given. No.951 was bought with two other engines as part of a 'package deal' and arrived at Ipswich in August 1984. All the headaches and frustration suddenly seemed worthwhile! The locomotive, which was restored in BR black livery as No.90775, is seen on the outskirts of Alton with a Santa special to Medstead in December 1986.   *Alan Chandler*

The crew of WD 2-10-0 No.90775 are evidently intent on gaining as much momentum as possible for the climb that lies ahead as it storms out of Alton towards Butts Junction in March 1987. The steeply-sided, deep cutting of the kind seen here is characteristic of many on the line. This was a double track section of line as far as Butts Junction. Not many photographers would consider taking a shot at such a tricky location, but it must have been the photographer's lucky day because the sun is shining and the smoke is clear of the locomotive. *Tony Eaton*

One of the most memorable days in the history of the MHR is 26th August 1987 when unrebuilt 'West Country' Class Pacific No.34105 *Swanage* and S15 Class 4-6-0 No.506 officially entered traffic. Both newly restored engines were launched into service during a special ceremony at Alresford station. After a short speech, during which he congratulated the volunteers involved in overhauling the engine, the Mayor of Swanage unveiled No.34105's nameplate to loud cheers and the clicking of cameras. The MHR's other principal guest was Mr Bob Urie, grandson of the famous locomotive designer R.W. Urie, who said his grandfather would have been very proud and pleased to see No.506 running again in her smart mid-1930s 'Southern' green livery. After the ceremony the locomotives made two runs to Alton and back conveying invited guests, and in the evening a further train was provided for the many volunteers who had worked so tirelessly over the years to restore the engines from Barry scrapyard condition. One of those workings is seen here between Alresford and Ropley. It should be noted that No.506 had been running in ordinary traffic since 8th July 1987, whilst No.34105 entered service on 23rd August.

Hugh Ballantyne

Two immaculate 'Southern' locomotives in BR livery, an arranged smoke effect, a uniform rake of coaches in green and, of course, that vital ingredient, bright autumn sunshine. What more could a railway photographer wish for? This picture shows the T9 Class 4-4-0 No.30120 piloting Bulleid 'West Country' Pacific No.34105 *Swanage* near Bighton Lane, between Alresford and Ropley, on 25th October 1987.

Roger Cruse

Most photographs taken on Medstead bank are, naturally, of trains toiling up the steep gradient towards Medstead & Four Marks station and it is unlikely that many pictures of trains coming down the bank are taken. But this illustration depicts the classic combination of the T9 piloting *Swanage* descending the bank with the 12.02pm Alresford to Alton train, also on 25th October 1987. Usually steam would be shut off at this point, but not on this occasion. Almost needless to say, the magnificent smoke and steam effects seen had been arranged in advance with the co-operative engine crews. *Graham Mallinson*

The shadows are lengthening at Medstead & Four Marks station as 'Austerity' 2-10-0 No.601 *Sturdee* draws to a halt with a 'Santa Special' train on 27th November 1988. This was the second day of running of these trains which operated between Alton and Medstead plus Alresford and Ropley. This locomotive, which initially ran on the MHR as No.90775, was repainted during the winter of 1987/88 in Longmoor Military Railway (LMR) blue livery and renumbered 601: it re-entered traffic on 4th April 1988. The original WD No.601 was named *Kitchener*, but the MHR's No.601 was named *Sturdee*, which was a family name of one of the owners. It certainly makes an absolutely splendid sight in the late afternoon sunshine. No.601 later left the MHR and, at the time of writing, can be seen on the North Norfolk Railway. War Department 'Austerity' locomotives had a much greater connection with the south of England than is commonly supposed. A fleet of 2-8-0s was allocated to the SR in the early 1950s and, in addition, the LMR's 2-10-0s regularly visited Eastleigh Works for repairs. *Sturdee*'s sister engine, No.600 *Gordon*, was the LMR's flagship locomotive for many years and sometimes appeared on rail tours on BR metals. It is now preserved at the Severn Valley Railway.

Alan Chandler

This photograph, which was taken in April 1989, shows No.506 easing away from Alton station in charge of a train to Alresford. The two platforms on the left, beyond the gate, are used by main line electric trains, whilst the MHR has sole use of the platform on the right of the picture. The water tower visible above the train came from Aldershot and was erected during the winter of 1987/88. Installation of the tower involved digging a 15ft. deep footing in the embankment which was then filled with concrete. The latter operation was complicated by the lack of road access to the site, and it was decided that the only solution would be to have ready mixed concrete delivered by lorry to Paper Mill Lane and then raised in a skip by the steam crane. This necessitated the partial closure of the road for safety reasons and the use of 'Stop/Go' boards. After this operation plumbing in the tower and arranging suitable drainage may have seemed like the easy part of the job!

Ian Wright

Left, above: Maunsell S15 Class 4-6-0 No.506 pulls an Alresford-bound train up the unrelenting 1 in 60 gradient through Chawton Wood on a glorious June day in the late 1980s. Chawton Park Wood (this is the wood's full name) is one of the highlights of a journey on the MHR. The wood extends to 516 acres, and the main part was purchased by the Forestry Commission in 1949 after it was felled. It lies on high ground, up to a height of 700ft. above sea level and the old Pilgrims Way from Canterbury to Salisbury passed through it. In the early 1950s the wood was replanted with a mixture of conifers and broadleaf trees. Not surprisingly, it is a haven for wildlife and sixty-six species of birds have been observed.

Ian Wright

Left, below: BR Standard Class 4MT 2-6-0 No.76017 heads an eastbound train near Ropley on 26th November 1989. Like so many BR Standard locomotives No.76017 had a tragically short working life. It was built at Horwich Works in Lancashire in June 1953, initially based at Eastleigh shed, and saw service on the Didcot, Newbury and Southampton line. The engine hit the headlines when, on 22nd September 1954, it was unable to stop at Whitchurch Town whilst powering a down freight and became derailed at the southern end of the station. Following repair it was normally found working both passenger and freight traffic between Portsmouth and Salisbury. In March 1960 No.76017 moved to Salisbury shed and sometimes worked to Bournemouth via Fordingbridge. It was withdrawn in July 1965 and sent to Barry for scrap after accumulating a paltry 496,834 miles. In 1972 a group of enthusiasts formed the Standard Four Locomotive Group with the aim of purchasing No.76017. In January 1974 it left Barry for (what is now called) the Buckinghamshire Railway Centre at Quainton Road, near Aylesbury. A move to the MHR occurred in 1978 and the locomotive eventually entered traffic on 19th May 1984. *Alan Chandler*

A real winter's day on the Mid Hants! With fresh overnight snow still clinging to the branches of trees, BR Standard Class 4MT 2-6-0 No.76017 sets off from Medstead station through The Shrave cutting with a three-coach train from Alresford in January 1991. A true Christmas card scene. *Ian Wright*

Swanage makes an all-out effort, and produces a memorable smoke effect, as it charges up the fierce 1 in 80 gradient towards Ropley with a Christmas train in December 1991. This locomotive was one of the last of the class to be built and was actually constructed in BR days, emerging from Brighton Works in March 1950. Two major events in the locomotive's career are noteworthy: on 3rd May 1951 it inaugurated the 'Royal Wessex' from Weymouth to Waterloo, whilst, less auspiciously on 2nd September 1959, it unfortunately disgraced itself when its oil bath caught fire. No.34105 was withdrawn from traffic in October 1964 after running 623,405 miles and was despatched to Barry scrapyard in February 1965. The group that purchased No.34105 for preservation had originally set out to buy a Stanier 8F but was unsuccessful and turned its attention to *Swanage* instead, which arrived on the Mid Hants line in March 1978. The locomotive made its debut in Mid Hants passenger service, as previously mentioned, on 23rd August 1987. After years of hard work tackling the line's demanding gradients, No.34105 was reported to be completely worn out by the summer of 1997 and remains out of service awaiting its turn for a general overhaul.

Tony Eaton

In early 1993 BR Standard Class 7P6F Pacific No.70000 *Britannia* visited the MHR and is seen here disguised as sister engine No.70004 *William Shakespeare*: it was photographed on 31st January near Bishops Sutton. Despite the dull conditions the locomotive certainly makes a fine sight carrying the full 'Golden Arrow' regalia, recalling the great days of this famous train. Earlier the same month 'No.70004', complete with 'Golden Arrow' embellishments, astonished morning commuters at Alton when it arrived from Clapham Junction at 7.30am!

There was a special mystique and magic about the 'Golden Arrow' – a service still remembered with affection by many people. No.70004 was one of two 'Britannia' Pacifics (the other was No.70014 *Iron Duke*) based at Stewarts Lane shed, Battersea, their principal duty being powering the 'Arrow' between Victoria and Dover Marine. Regrettably, in 1958 the two Pacifics were transferred to Trafford Park shed, Manchester, for use on London expresses via the Midland route and soon lost their shine.

David Clark

Left, above: Pacific No.70000 *Britannia* has made several visits to the MHR and, in this shot, is seen in full cry between Ropley and Medstead, brightening up an otherwise dreary day. This picture was taken in March 1993. *Britannia* performed at the twentieth anniversary of the BR closure gala 'weekend' during February and finally departed on 19th March. The locomotive returned in October 1993 to participate in the 'Standards Weekend' and further visits were made in May 1994, when it arrived with a rail tour from Waterloo, and for the autumn 1994 'Enthusiasts Weekend' when it ran as No.70014 *Iron Duke*. *Ian Wright*

Left, below: The MHR probably suffered a rise in its coal bill during the early part of May 1993 and the reason was not difficult to fathom: two unrebuilt Bulleid Pacifics were at large on the line! These locomotives were notoriously 'heavy on coal' but most enthusiasts would contend that an increase in the coal bill was a small price to pay for the magnificent sight of these two highly distinctive machines charging up and down the line. No doubt the extra fuel costs were balanced by an increase in custom. In this illustration Nos.34072 *257 Squadron* (on loan from the Swanage Railway) and 34105 *Swanage* climb past Chawton Wood with the 2.15pm Alton to Alresford train on the 1st May 1993. *David Cox*

Another picture of the magnificent Bulleid duo. This shot, which was taken on May 2nd, the day after the previous picture, depicts *Swanage* leading *257 Squadron* through Chawton Wood, with both engines emitting clouds of black smoke. Note the improvement in the weather conditions, the sun shining brightly as the two locomotives pass the photographer. By this time *Swanage* had been in service for almost six years and its paintwork had lost much of its 'gleam', thus adding to the realism of this illustration. The pairing of two unrebuilt Bulleid Pacifics has, as far as the author is aware, only occurred three times in the preservation era, so these shots are of considerable historical interest.

Roger Cruse

Left, above: A powerful photograph of a powerful locomotive! Displaying a special headboard to mark the 20th anniversary of the Mid Hants Railway, Bulleid 'Merchant Navy' Class No.35005 *Canadian Pacific* assaults the bank between Alresford and Ropley on 4th July 1993. Constructed as No.21C5 at Eastleigh Works in December 1941, *Canadian Pacific* was among the first of its class to enter traffic. It was renumbered in April 1948 and re-entered service after rebuilding in May 1959. The locomotive was withdrawn in October 1965 and sent to Barry scrapyard. In addition to its exploits on the Mid Hants line, No.35005 has been a regular performer on the main line.

Hugh Ballantyne

Left, below: BR Standard Class 9F 2-10-0 No.92203 *Black Prince* threads Chawton Wood at the head of an Alresford-bound train in May 1994. This locomotive was rescued from the scrapman's torch by David Shepherd, the well-known artist, and is currently based at Toddington on the Gloucestershire Warwickshire Railway. This was the first visit of a Class 9F to the Mid Hants line in preservation, but not the first time a member of this class had passed over the line. On 20th September 1964 the virtual end of steam working on the Waterloo to Exeter line was commemorated by the 'Farewell to Steam Tour' organised by the Southern Counties Touring Society. Fittingly, haulage was by the final steam locomotive to be built by BR, Class 9F No.92220 *Evening Star*. The special started in London and travelled down the Mid Hants line before running to Salisbury via Southampton. The train's destination was Seaton, but it is most unlikely that *Evening Star* worked throughout!

Ian Wright

Photographed at the same spot as the previous picture, BR Standard Class 5MT No.73096, which was running at that time in black livery as No.73080 *Merlin*, storms up Medstead bank with the 1.30pm Alton to Alresford train on 4th February 1995. Following release from Derby Works in December 1955, No.73096 began its BR career working from Patricroft shed, Manchester, which later became famous as one of BR's last steam depots. In August 1958 the Standard moved to Shrewsbury, seeing use on the scenic Central Wales line, before moving back to the LMR in November 1964. By a strange quirk of fate its working life finished at Patricroft, in November 1967, after a pathetically brief career, but this was typical of many steam locomotives at this time. No.73096 arrived on the MHR from Barry Island on 10th July 1985, becoming the 164th engine to leave for a better life after residing there since February 1968. During its restoration the manufacture of a new tender body and overhaul of the boiler were carried out by contractors and No.73096 eventually returned to service in 1993. Another milestone in the locomotive's life was reached on 15th February 1998 when it hauled the inaugural run of the 'Daylight Limited' series of rail tours on the national system which took participants to Salisbury. During the return run No.73096 ran like an engine possessed, topping Savernake summit at no less than 68mph, a truly remarkable performance.

David Cox

One of the highlights of 1993 at the MHR was the appearance in February of (then) recently restored LSWR M7 Class 0-4-4T No.30053 and it came as no surprise when a further visit was arranged for the spring of 1995. The M7 is depicted on a chartered freight train on 13th March 1995. One of 105 of these locomotives built between 1897-1911 for branch line and secondary passenger work, No.30053 was among the last survivors, based at Bournemouth shed for working the Lymington and Swanage branch trains. The engine was withdrawn in May 1964, but specially retained to work a rail tour in the London area after which it was dumped at Nine Elms shed awaiting disposal. In December 1964 it was purchased for preservation in the United States and shipped out in 1966. But that was not the end of the story! In the early 1980s a group of British enthusiasts associated with the Swanage Railway discovered that No.30053's owner might be prepared to sell the engine and after lengthy negotiations it arrived at Felixstowe docks on 6th April 1987. Early efforts towards restoration were carried out at Swindon, but the group had to leave its base there and work later continued at the East Anglian Railway Museum, near Colchester. The climax of the M7's thorough and painstaking overhaul came on 29th April 1992 when it moved for the first time for many years under its own steam. No.30053 is normally based at Swanage, but at the time of writing is dismantled for a major overhaul. *Roger Whitehead*

The visit of No.30053 provided a golden opportunity to recreate a Mid Hants branch line train of the early 1950s as seen here in this shot of a photographers' charter train descending Medstead bank through Chawton Wood on 14th March 1995. No.30053 had been renumbered 30479, this being one of the M7 Class engines that were particularly associated with the line in times gone by. Normally locomotives would be 'shut off' going down the bank so, to add life to the picture, smoke effects were specially provided by the locomotive's crew. Everything was arranged with considerable attention to detail enabling photographers to obtain a picture of which they could be proud, and even the sun deigned to shine!   *Roger Cruse*

In this almost perfect recreation of a Southern Region branch line scene, the crew of 'No.30479' relax on a platform seat at Alton station as their locomotive simmers gently beside them. In former days Platform 3 at Alton was used by Meon Valley line trains, whilst Platform 2 was normally the preserve of workings on the Mid Hants line, so the purists would no doubt argue that this shot is not historically correct. Even so, a truly evocative image has resulted. Unfortunately, by the time the MHR opened, all of the vintage LSWR coaches in BR service had, regrettably, long since been withdrawn, so Bulleid brake coach No.S4211 was used instead, plus a BR Standard vehicle.

Roger Cruse

Right above: The operation of a preserved railway is a hugely expensive business, even when the vast majority of the staff are volunteers, and most heritage lines arrange a variety of special events to attract extra passengers. In this illustration Alresford station forecourt appears to be the venue for a car boot sale and presumably some of the stallholders and customers took the opportunity to have a ride on the train. The most popular events with the general public at the MHR are undoubtedly the 'Days out with Thomas' extravaganzas and 'Santa Specials' during the run-up to Christmas. Railway enthusiasts are also well catered for, with a range of special steam and diesel weekend galas, often with visiting locomotives. In this picture Bulleid Pacific No.34105 *Swanage*, running as No.34051 *Winston Churchill* poses at Alresford on 1st July 1995. The 'real' No.34051 is preserved by the National Railway Museum. *John Scrace*

Right below: The controversial sight of Bulleid 'Merchant Navy' Pacific No.35005 *Canadian Pacific* in blue no doubt provoked strong opinions from people in favour and those against such a livery. But surely they could all agree on one thing – at least it was different! In the very early days of the BR regime, blue was used as an experimental locomotive livery, but did not find favour with the hierarchy: it was never carried by a rebuilt Bulleid Pacific. Here, *Canadian Pacific* is depicted near Chawton on 16th June 1996. *David Clark*

Maunsell U Class 2-6-0 No.31625, in exemplary condition, works a freight train charter near Chawton Wood on 14th September 1996, the day after it returned to service. This locomotive was built at Ashford in 1929 for mixed traffic duties and led an uneventful life until it was converted to oil burning in 1947: it was re-converted during the following year. The locomotive was withdrawn from BR service in January 1964 with a total mileage of 1,063,982 and despatched to Barry six months later. It was bought privately for preservation and arrived on the MHR in March 1980. The engine's restoration to working condition was considerably helped by the fact that it had received an extensive rebuild in 1961 which apparently included new frames, wheelsets and cylinders; the locomotive was in quite reasonable shape mechanically despite its sixteen year sojourn at Barry. Another bonus was the generally satisfactory condition of the boiler. No.31625 returned to steam on 13th September 1996 after an extremely thorough overhaul to main line standard, including the fitting of Automatic Warning System (AWS) equipment. Exactly a year later to the day No.31625 made its debut on the main line as a preserved locomotive powering 'The Severn Venturer' rail tour from London to Bristol and back, reportedly 'running like a sewing machine'. It has since made further sorties on to the main line, including an appearance at 'Steam on the Met'.   *Stuart Hammond*

The Maunsell 'Moguls' were built, as previously stated, for mixed traffic work which included secondary passenger trains similar to that seen here in this lovely picture of No.31625 leaving Alresford on a brilliantly bright and sunny 15th February 1997. The scene rekindles memories of the much-lamented Midland & South Western Junction line which connected Andover and Cheltenham. This classic rural back-water, which lost its passenger trains in September 1961, was a haunt of Maunsell 'Moguls' usually hauling three-coach trains – though it should be added that the stock was normally of GWR origin.   *Roger Cruse*

Flaming June on the Mid Hants Railway! A brace of Maunsell 'Moguls' – N Class No.31874 and U Class No.31625 – run through Medstead & Four Marks station with a photographic charter train on 27th June 1997. This picture was taken from the new footbridge that came from Cowes station on the Isle of Wight. The bridge was opened to the public on 28th August 1996 and was yet another milestone in the unbelievable transformation of Medstead station, which was virtually in ruins when the Mid Hants Railway took over. In 1997 the quality of the work carried out on the bridge was officially recognised when the MHR was awarded a Certificate of Excellence by the Ian Allan National Railway Heritage Awards scheme.

David Cox

Savour the atmosphere of an English summer's day! Hauling the train seen in the previous picture, Nos.31874 and 31625 enter Alresford station after a summer downpour. The wet weather conditions, with rain-soaked track and puddles on the platforms, have at least given a different dimension to this picture. *David Cox*

Photographed during the 'Salute to the Southern' event which was held during the first weekend of July 1997, Maunsell 'Mogul' No.31874 (running in the guise of No.31873) and pilot engine No.31625 simmer at the west end of Ropley station on 6th July 1997. This event was organised to commemorate the thirtieth anniversary of the end of steam on the Southern Region and doubtless rekindled happy memories for many enthusiasts. To add a touch of realism the weekend featured locomotives with tear-jerking slogans, such as 'The End' and 'Don't Let Me Die', chalked on their smokebox doors, these being similar to those seen at the time of SR steam's demise. No.34105 *Swanage* was disguised for the event (as previously mentioned), becoming No.34102 *Lapford*, which was the last unrebuilt Bulleid Pacific in BR operation. BR Standard Class 4MT No.76017, minus coupling rods and bearing suitable chalked inscriptions, was towed off to an imaginary scrap yard!   *David Cox*

When Urie S15 Class No.506 entered service on the MHR in 1987 following its restoration from a Barry 'wreck' it sported 'Southern' green livery and ran in this condition for some years. However, a decision was taken to repaint the locomotive into BR black and it made its debut in this livery on 7th February 1993. In the mid-1990s further work was undertaken on No.30506 (as No.506 had become) involving an exchange of boilers with sister engine No.30499, and it returned to service on 1st March 1997. Later that year, on 22nd November, No.30506 was employed on a freight train charter and is seen here at North Street, near Ropley.
Stuart Hammond

Urie S15 No.30506 creates a truly evocative image climbing towards Ropley with the freight train charter seen in the previous shot. The attention of most railway enthusiasts tends to focus on locomotives and there is no doubt that No.30506 is a fine machine, but the train's rake of wagons should not be ignored. A huge amount of time and effort (not to mention money) has obviously been expended on restoring the fine assortment of wagons to their former glory. The humble railway wagon was for generations the backbone of the railway system and should not be overlooked!

Stuart Hammond

The Mid Hants line has some substantial earthworks, most notably very deep cuttings, excavation of which must have presented a huge challenge to the navvies building the line. But here is an illustration of a different earthwork, the massive embankment that is a major feature of the line near North Street, between Ropley and Medstead stations. Here Urie S15 Class No.30506 strides across the high embankment with an Alresford to Alton train on a crisp December day in 1997. Hopefully, passengers were enjoying the panoramic view of the surrounding countryside.

Tony Eaton

On a fine early spring morning Ivatt 2-6-2T No.41312 and BR Standard Class 5MT No.73096 – a most unusual combination – team up to head a train out of Alton. They were photographed ascending Medstead bank on 1st March 1999. The trees on the right of the shot, which stand at one of the lineside photographers' favourite locations, appear in many illustrations in this book and must surely be some of the most-photographed railway lineside trees in the country!

Tony Eaton

The Mid Hants Railway's incomparable ability to recreate the last days of BR steam is exemplified in this portrait of Ivatt Class 2MT 2-6-2T No.41312. The picture could easily be mistaken for the southern section of the Somerset & Dorset line, but the location is actually near Ropley. The 'Ivatt' is seen heading down the bank towards Alresford during a photographic charter on 13th November 1999.   *David Cox*

Photographed in dramatic evening lighting conditions, No.41312 is depicted near Chawton Wood with a charter freight on 13th November 1999. No.41312 was outshopped from Crewe Works in May 1952 and was one of a class of 130 locomotives, most of which were scattered around the London Midland Region for branch and secondary line duties. No.41312, however, was a member of a batch earmarked for use on the SR, spending time in Kent before being moved to Barnstaple Junction in January 1960 for working the long-lost Torrington and Ilfracombe lines. It later saw service at Brighton and Bournemouth sheds, powering trains on the last day of steam on the Lymington branch. The locomotive's final BR duties involved empty stock working into and out of Waterloo. Rescued from Barry in 1974, No.41312 was stabled at the Gwili Railway, near Carmarthen, until coming to the MHR in October 1995. Restoration to working order was speedy and achieved in only three years, but the work undertaken was nonetheless extensive. Due to corrosion new side tanks, cab sides and roof had to be manufactured, while the bunker needed a new front sheet complete with tool lockers. No.41312 moved under its own power for the first time in preservation on 30th December 1998. It has since become a roving ambassador for the MHR, visiting no fewer than six preserved railways since restoration.

David Cox

Rebuilt Bulleid 'West Country' Pacific No.34016 *Bodmin* runs past the photographer with a charter train on 12th November 2000. This picture was taken below Medstead & Four Marks when the train was heading downhill towards Ropley with steam on, so is a most unorthodox view. *Bodmin*, which was (as previously mentioned) the MHR's flagship locomotive for many years, was constructed at Brighton Works in November 1945 and originally numbered 21C116. It was renumbered 34016 by the newly-created BR in July 1948. No.34016 was rebuilt at Eastleigh Works in April 1958 and the high point of its career was probably attained a few weeks later hauling a special train for the President of Italy and his wife from Dover to Victoria. No.34016 was withdrawn in June 1964 after covering 811,674 miles and sold to Woodhams of Barry for cutting-up. Mercifully, this did not occur and *Bodmin* was saved for preservation in 1971, restoration taking place initially at Quainton Road in Buckinghamshire. In November 1976 No.34016 was moved to the MHR and eventually returned to steam in September 1979, after an estimated 30,000 man-hours were spent working on the engine. *Bodmin* ran more than 40,000 miles before being withdrawn for overhaul in 1990. It was dismantled in 1991, but the repair was delayed by lack of finance. An appeal fund was set up to raise £42,000 to complete the work with the happy result that *Bodmin* worked a test train to Salisbury on 10th June 2000 and put in a sparkling performance during which it topped Savernake summit at 68mph equalling No.73096's run in February 1998.   *David Cox*

During the last week of September 2003 the MHR staged a steam gala with guest locomotives from the Bluebell, Nene Valley, Severn Valley and Swanage Railways. MHR-based locomotives are not exactly prominent in this shot(!) which shows LBSCR Class E4 0-6-2T No.473 *Birch Grove*, from the Bluebell Railway, receiving some last-minute attention in Ropley shed yard on 28th September 2003, flanked by BR Standard 2-6-4T No.80104 from the Swanage Railway. Also in the picture is (what appears to be) the tender of 'Black Five' No.45379. This locomotive has since been purchased by the MHR. The star attraction during the three-day event was LNER Class A4 Pacific No.60009 *Union of South Africa* from the Severn Valley Railway.

David Cox

Another picture taken during the September 2003 steam gala. Unfortunately the event was somewhat marred by the failure of unrebuilt Bulleid 'Battle of Britain' Class No.34081 *92 Squadron* from the Nene Valley Railway, which is depicted in Ropley yard on 28th September. Despite being out of steam, it still manages to create a stirring sight in early BR livery. The two other engines visible need no introduction!

David Cox

In March 2004 the MHR organised a steam gala with a 'South Western branch' theme and the visiting locomotives included the dainty Beattie Class 0298 2-4-0WT No.30587. This diminutive machine, which is part of the National Collection, is based on the Bodmin & Wenford Railway in Cornwall. It was photographed leaving Alresford hauling a short freight train on 9th March. This delightful locomotive was built by Beyer Peacock for working suburban trains out of Waterloo in 1874, so it really is quite a veteran! A total of eighty-five locomotives were built between 1863 and 1875, but only three survived to see the 20th century and were rebuilt by successive chief mechanical engineers. They were retained at Wadebridge shed, in Cornwall, to work china clay traffic along the Wenford Bridge branch and lasted on this work until the early 1960s. Happily, two of the survivors were saved for posterity.

Roger Cruse

A thrilling sight for every 'Southern' enthusiast! Visiting Bulleid 'West Country' Pacific No.34027 *Taw Valley*, running as No.34045 *Ottery St. Mary*, pilots sister engine No.34016 *Bodmin* through Chawton Wood during a steam gala on 19th September 2004.   *Roger Cruse*

Finale! *Bodmin*, surely one of the most impressive and best-loved preserved locomotives in Great Britain, glints in the evening sun. A November 2000 picture.
Stuart Hammond